...ker

...oves ...t he ..., even ...ts

Philippa Feltpen

A real peacemaker, she helps keep the other Pens in order by sorting out arguments and giving good advice.

Waxy Max

He's very sporty and football mad. On the outside, he's tough, but underneath he's got the biggest heart.

Splodge, do you like swings?

Squiggle and Splodge

The Scribble twins! They're both quiet, both shy. Although they may not look alike, they do almost everything together.

Enter ...

Pens

Helping you to get to know God more

Sorry God

Written by

Alexa Tewkesbury

Every day a short Bible reading is brought to life with the help of the Pens characters. A related question and prayer apply this to daily life. Written in four sections, two focusing on the lives of Pens and two on Bible characters, young children will be inspired to learn more of God and His Word.

What's inside?

CWR

Day 1

RIGHT FROM WRONG

'Never boast about tomorrow. You don't know what will happen between now and then.' (Proverbs 27 v 1)

Mountain Pens

Someone was knocking loudly on Denzil's front door.

'Good morning!' boomed a voice. It was Heidi, Henry Highlighter's auntie. Heidi Highlighter was taking Denzil, Marco, Max and Sharpy on a mountain-climbing trip!

'We'll start with a small mountain,' she explained. 'A mountain you can walk up. Then, as you get fitter and stronger, you'll be able to try proper mountain climbing. That's when you'll need special equipment to help you, like ropes and helmets.'

Marco looked disappointed.

'I could do proper mountain climbing now,' he boasted. 'On my own! I'm stronger and fitter and BRAVER than anyone!'

God doesn't want us to boast. He wants us to trust in Him.

The things we're good at are called 'talents' or 'gifts'. Who has given them to us?

Pens Prayer

Father God, thank You for helping me to learn to do so many things. Please teach me not to be boastful. Amen.

Day 2 Right from Wrong

'The LORD says, "… If you will only obey me …"'
(Isaiah 1 vv 18–19)

Mountain campers

At the foot of the mountain, Heidi said, 'Let's make camp.'

So Marco, Max and Denzil set up the tents. Then Heidi checked that they were fixed firmly to the ground.

'We don't want the wind blowing them away!' she laughed. 'Now, let's have supper and get to bed. We need lots of energy to walk up the mountain tomorrow.'

'But *I* could walk up it *now*,' moaned Marco. 'All by myself.'

'That's silly,' replied Denzil. 'You've never been up a mountain before. You need Heidi to help you. We all do.'

'Not me!' chirped Marco. 'I'm Marco-the-mountaineer!'

We need to try to obey God so that He can keep us safe.

Why is it important for Marco to do as Heidi tells him?

Pens Prayer

Dear Lord, thank You so much for taking care of me. Amen.

Day 3

Right from Wrong

'... you should decide never to do anything that would make another ... fall into sin.' (Romans 14 v 13)

Mountain morning

Next morning, Marco was awake early. Everyone else was still asleep.

'I'm going to show Denzil that he's wrong,' Marco thought to himself. 'I don't need Heidi's help. I'm going to climb the mountain all by myself.'

But, as Marco opened the tent, Denzil woke up.

'Where are you going?' Denzil asked.

'I'm going to climb the mountain,' Marco whispered.

'No!' muttered Denzil. 'It's not safe. You must wait for Heidi.'

Marco wasn't listening. He was already outside.

But Denzil couldn't let him go by himself. He got dressed quickly. Then he followed Marco to the mountain.

Doing silly, wrong or dangerous things sometimes leads other people to do them, too.

Denzil follows Marco to try to help him. What should he have done instead?

Pens Prayer

Lord God, please help me to make good choices in the things I do by following Your instructions in the Bible. Amen.

Day 4 Right from Wrong

'... watch what you do!' (Luke 17 v 3)

Mountain fog

When Max and Sharpy got up, the air was cold and misty.

'Let's go and wake Marco and Denzil,' Max shivered.

Outside his friends' tent, he called, 'Helloo!'

There was no answer.

'Wakey wakey!' Max said. 'It's breakfast time.'

But the tent was empty!

Max and Heidi looked all around but there was no sign of the missing Pens.

'Oh dear!' frowned Heidi. 'I hope they haven't gone walking up the mountain on their own. It's too dangerous. And now it's getting foggy. They'll get lost! They won't be able to find their way back down again.'

God is sad when we don't listen to Him and we leave Him out. He wants to look after us.

When the weather is foggy, what is it hard to do?

Pens Prayer

Father, I'm sorry for the times when I leave You out. I want to remember You every day. Amen.

Day 5

Right from Wrong

'... those who do not do the good they know they should do are guilty of sin.' (James 4 v 17)

Mountain trouble

Marco and Denzil were getting cold. It was foggy, too. They couldn't see very far in front of them. They couldn't see very far behind them either.

'It wasn't foggy when we left and we were following a path,' Marco frowned. 'Now I can't even see if there's a path or not.'

'This is all your fault!' snapped Denzil. 'Why didn't you wait for Heidi?'

'You didn't have to follow me,' grumbled Marco.

'Well, I couldn't let you go on your own!' cried Denzil. 'And now we're *both* in trouble!'

Doing the wrong thing can hurt other people as well as ourselves.

How do you think Marco feels now that he and Denzil are lost?

Pens Prayer

Dear Lord, please teach me always to know right from wrong. Amen.

Day 6 Right from Wrong

'You are good to us and forgiving, full of constant love for all who pray to you.' (Psalm 86 v 5)

Mountain searchers

At the foot of the mountain, Heidi called: 'Marco! Denzil!'

Beside her, Max called, too: 'Denzil! Marco!'

Sharpy pricked up his ears to listen.

But no one answered. Everything was quiet in the thick fog.

'There's nothing else for it,' said Heidi. 'We'll have to walk up the mountain until we find them.'

Max was cross. 'If they hadn't gone off on their own, they wouldn't be lost,' he grumbled.

'I know,' agreed Heidi. 'But now they need our help. We must do everything we can to get them safely back down again.'

Even when we do things that are wrong, God never stops wanting to help us.

If someone upsets you or makes you cross, what does God hope you'll do?

Pens Prayer

Father God, please help me to forgive other people the way You always forgive me. Amen.

Day 7 Right from Wrong

'Some … could not find their way … Then in their trouble they called to the LORD … (Psalm 107 vv 4,6)

Mountain shouting

Marco was worried.

Denzil was scared.

'I think we should start walking back down the mountain,' Marco said.

'No,' Denzil answered. 'We should stay where we are until the fog clears. Then we'll be able to find the path again.'

'But I'm cold,' moaned Marco. 'And I'm *really* hungry.'

'So am I,' grunted Denzil.

Marco sniffed. 'I'm sorry, Denzil,' he said. 'I didn't mean to get you into trouble.'

'I know,' smiled Denzil. 'I tell you what, let's shout for help. As loudly as we can. Someone's sure to hear us in the end.'

When we call out to God and tell Him we're sorry, He will always hear us.

Do you think Pens should start walking down the mountain, or wait for the fog to clear?

Pens Prayer

Lord God, thank You that when I say sorry to You for doing wrong things, You always forgive me. Amen.

Day 8 Right from Wrong

'... [God's] love is eternal and his faithfulness lasts for ever.' (Psalm 100 v 5)

Mountain rescuers

Heidi, Max and Sharpy set off up the mountain. Heidi had climbed it lots of times before. It was still foggy, but she knew the right way to go.

Suddenly Sharpy stopped.

His nose was twitching.

Then he began to trot away from the path.

'No, Sharpy!' called Heidi. 'You must stay with us.'

'But Sharpy's sniffing,' said Max. 'Perhaps his nose is telling him where Marco and Denzil are. I think we should follow him. Sharpy's sense of smell is never wrong.'

'Are you sure?' frowned Heidi.

'Oh, yes!' replied Max. 'I trust Sharpy's nose completely.'

If we love God, we can trust Him to help us when we need Him.

Our sense of smell is one of our five senses. Do you know the others?

Pens Prayer

Thank You for loving me, God, today, tomorrow and always. Amen.

Day 9 Right from Wrong

'… if we confess our sins to God, he will keep his promise and … forgive us …' (1 John 1 v 9)

Mountain friends

Snuffle, snuffle … Sharpy sniffed his way across the mountainside.

Suddenly …

'What was that?' hissed Max.

Then his eyes lit up. He and Heidi could hear voices.

Voices belonging to Marco and Denzil!

'I knew we could trust Sharpy's nose!' cried Max.

Marco and Denzil were SO pleased to see them.

'I'm sorry I was boastful,' said Marco. 'I'm sorry I got Denzil into trouble and didn't do as I was told. Thanks for coming to find us.'

'You didn't really think we'd leave you up a mountain, did you?' beamed Max. 'Come on. Let's go home.'

Saying sorry to God means that He can forgive us, and we can be close to Him again.

Do you sometimes find it hard to say sorry? Ask God to help you.

Pens Prayer

Thank You, dear Father, that I belong to You and You will never let me go. Amen.

ELIJAH-THE-GOOD

When God stopped the rain

Day 10

'In the name of the LORD ... I tell you that there will be no dew or rain ...' (1 Kings 17 v 1)

God's message

The king of Israel was called Ahab.

King Ahab took no notice of God and was not His friend.

He didn't obey God.

He did lots of things that made God sad.

Many of God's people began to do things that made God sad, too.

But God had a friend called Elijah. God told Elijah to give the king a message.

So Elijah went to King Ahab and said, 'God has asked me to tell you this: there won't be any more rain here until you start to listen to Him.'

God loves us, but the selfish things we sometimes do make Him sad.

Pens Prayer

Father God, as I grow bigger, I want to love You more and more. Amen.

Elijah-the-Good

When God stopped the rain

Day 11

'The brook will supply you with water to drink, and I have commanded ravens to bring you food ... ' (1 Kings 17 v 4)

God saves Elijah

God's friend, Elijah, had done just as God asked him to. God was pleased with him.

So God said, 'Listen, Elijah. Without any rain, there will be no food here. There won't be any water left to drink either. But you have obeyed me and I'm going to take care of you. Go away from here and hide by Cherith stream. You can drink the water from there. And you won't be hungry,' God added. 'I'll make sure that ravens bring you food.'

Again, Elijah did exactly as God told him to.

God could look after Elijah because Elijah listened to Him.

Pens Prayer

Please help me to do good and to obey You, dear Lord, just like Elijah. Amen.

Elijah-the-Good

When God stopped the rain

Day 12

'After a while the brook dried up because of the lack of rain.' (1 Kings 17 v 7)

Down by the stream, Elijah was safe. There was water for him to drink. Then, every morning and evening, ravens brought him food – just as God had said they would.

But, because it didn't rain, one day the water in the stream dried up.

'Don't worry,' God said to Elijah. 'Go to a town called Zarephath. A woman lives there whose husband has died. She will give you food and water.'

God knew that Elijah was a good man who loved Him. So God went on taking care of him.

Elijah trusted God and wanted to please Him.

Pens Prayer

Lord God, Elijah's story shows me how You take care of Your friends. Thank You. Amen.

Elijah-the-Good
When God stopped the rain

Day 13

'... as [Elijah] came to the gate of the town, he saw a widow gathering firewood.' (1 Kings 17 v 10)

The woman with the wood

When Elijah arrived in Zarephath, he saw the woman God had told him about. She was collecting firewood.

'Hello,' Elijah said. 'Please may I have some water? I'm very thirsty.' Then he added, 'I'm hungry, too. Do you have any bread?'

The woman shook her head sadly. 'No,' she answered. 'I have a little flour and a tiny drop of oil. That's all. I was just getting some wood to make a fire. Then I'll bake them into bread for myself and my son. After that, I don't know what to do,' she shrugged. 'It'll be our last meal.'

The woman had no food for Elijah. But Elijah knew that God wouldn't let him down.

Pens Prayer

Loving Lord, thank You that You always keep Your promises to us. Amen.

Day 14

'... the LORD ... says: "The bowl will not run out of flour or the jar run out of oil ..."' (1 Kings 17 v 14)

Elijah's Smile

Elijah smiled at the woman kindly.

'Everything will be all right,' he said. 'Go and cook your meal. But, first of all, make something for me. Just a small loaf of bread. Then bake the rest for yourself and your son.'

The woman stared at Elijah. She watched as his smile grew even wider. Elijah was smiling because God had given him a message for her. 'God wants you to know something,' Elijah beamed. 'Your flour and oil won't run out before He makes it rain again. And that's a promise from God Himself.'

God promises good things to those who listen to Him.

Pens Prayer

Dear God, please teach me to listen to You as I read the Bible and learn more about You. Amen.

Elijah-the-Good

When God stopped the rain

Day 15

'The widow went and did as Elijah had told her ...' (1 Kings 17 v 15)

Plenty!

The woman could hardly believe her ears! Was God really speaking to her?

She hurried off to do as Elijah had said. First, she baked some bread for him. Then she mixed the flour and oil left over to make bread for her son and herself. There was plenty for all three of them.

The next day, the woman found that there was *still* plenty of flour and oil to bake more bread.

And the day after that.

In fact, they all had enough to eat for a very long time. Just as God had promised they would.

God loves to take care of His friends.

Pens Prayer

Lord God, thank You for always doing what's best for me. Help me to do my best for You. Amen.

Day 16 GOD HAS FEELINGS, TOO

'... love is not ill-mannered or selfish or irritable ...'
(1 Corinthians 13 v 5)

Ready for the fair

Gloria, Philippa and Charlotte were taking Squiggle, Splodge and Rowena Rollerball to the fair.

'Hurry UP, Squiggle!' Splodge shrieked. She was very excited because Rowena was going with them.

'I'll be there in a minute,' called Squiggle. 'I can't find my purse.'

Splodge looked grumpy. 'Trust Squiggle,' she moaned to Rowena. 'She's *always* losing things.'

'That's not very kind, Splodge,' said Philippa. 'And I'm sure it's not true either. Now, instead of being grumpy with Squiggle, let's help her instead.'

God is pleased when we're patient with each other. He is patient with us, too.

What sort of things make you impatient?

Pens Prayer

Dear Lord, please help me to be kind and patient with my family and friends. Amen.

Day 17 God Has Feelings, Too

'What [the LORD] requires of us is this: … to show constant love …' (Micah 6 v 8)

At the fairground, Squiggle, Splodge and Rowena gazed around eagerly.

The rides were so colourful!

The music was so loud!

'Ooh!' squealed Splodge. 'What shall we have a go on first?'

Squiggle wanted to try the big swings.

Rowena wanted to try the huge slide.

'You go on the swings then, Squiggle,' decided Splodge. 'Rowena and I will go on the slide. Come on, Rowena!'

And off they ran.

'Shall I take you on the swings, Squiggle?' Gloria asked.

Squiggle looked sad. 'No, thank you,' she sighed. 'I don't want to go on them any more.'

When we make each other sad, God is sad, too.

Why do you think Squiggle looked sad?

Pens Prayer

Father God, I want to make other people happy, not sad. Please help me. Amen.

Day 18 God Has Feelings, Too

'So then, you must clothe yourselves with ... kindness ...'
(Colossians 3 v 12)

'Let's go on the merry-go-round and ride on the horses!' squeaked Splodge.

Squiggle, Splodge and Rowena ran across the grass. But when they got to the merry-go-round, it was nearly full. There were only two horses left.

'Come on, Rowena!' said Splodge. 'There's just room for us. See you in a minute, Squiggle,' she added. 'You can have a go when we come back.'

Squiggle watched Splodge and Rowena whirling round and round and up and down.

'Your turn, Squiggle,' said Splodge, when they got off.

'No, thank you,' answered Squiggle. 'I don't want a ride any more.'

When we leave someone out, God feels left out, too.

When Splodge saw that there were only two horses left, what would it have been kind to say to Squiggle?

Pens Prayer

Dear God, please help me to think about other people's feelings and not just my own. Amen.

Day 19 God Has Feelings, Too

'... look out for one another's interests, not just for your own.' (Philippians 2 v 4)

Thirsty Pens

'I'm so thirsty!' cried Rowena Rollerball.

'Me, too,' answered Splodge.

'And me,' chirped Squiggle.

'Let's stop for a moment,' suggested Charlotte. 'Then you can all have a drink.'

Philippa gave Squiggle and Splodge some apple juice. Rowena had brought a carton of strawberry milkshake.

'I've got a spare straw,' Rowena said. 'Would anyone like to try my milkshake?'

'Me! Me! Me!' squeaked Splodge, before Squiggle had time to say anything.

'What about you, Squiggle?' asked Rowena.

Squiggle shrugged, 'No, thank you. Splodge can try it. I don't really want to.'

When we put ourselves first and other people last, we put God last, too.

What's your favourite drink?

Pens Prayer

Father, I don't want to be selfish. Please help me to try to put other people first. Amen.

Day 20 God Has Feelings, Too

'... let us be happy, let us celebrate!' (Psalm 118 v 24)

Coconuts

3

Splodge spotted a row of posts. Each one had a coconut sitting on top.

'That's the coconut shy,' explained Philippa. 'You throw a ball at each coconut to try and knock it off its post.'

Squiggle, Splodge and Rowena tried – but not one coconut fell down.

'Philippa, you try!' they laughed.

So Philippa tried with one … two … three balls. She hit one … two … three coconuts! And she won one … two … three sticks of candyfloss – which she gave to Squiggle, Splodge and Rowena.

'Thank you, Philippa!' cried Splodge. 'I LOVE the fair!'

When we have fun together and make each other happy, we make God happy, too.

Have you ever seen a coconut? Do you know what's inside?

Pens Prayer

Lord God, thank You so much for giving me friends to enjoy happy times with. Amen.

Day 21 God Has Feelings, Too

'... love one another as brothers and sisters, and be kind and humble with one another.' (1 Peter 3 v 8)

At lunchtime, Philippa, Gloria and Charlotte spread a rug on the grass. Then they unpacked a picnic basket. There were sandwiches, crisps, carrot sticks and grapes.

When Pens had finished eating, there was just one bag of crisps left over.

'Who hasn't eaten their crisps?' asked Charlotte.

'Me!' giggled Splodge. 'I'm too excited to eat much today. Is anyone still hungry?'

'I am!' answered Squiggle and Rowena, both at the same time.

'Why don't we share them, Squiggle?' suggested Rowena.

'That's a good idea,' agreed Squiggle. 'I don't think I could eat another whole bag all by myself anyway.'

When we're generous and share with others, we are generous towards God, too.

As well as the fair, what other places are good for picnics?

Pens Prayer

Father God, please help me to be generous to other people the way You are generous to me. Amen.

Day 22 God Has Feelings, Too

'... do not make God's Holy Spirit sad ...' (Ephesians 4 v 30)

Bouncy Castle

'Look at the HUGE bouncy castle!' gasped Rowena.

'It's ENORMOUS!' laughed Splodge.

'I'm going to jump higher than everyone!' cried Squiggle.

Splodge held hands with Rowena so that they could jump up and down together. But when Squiggle tried to join in, they all lost their balance and fell over!

'Oops!' giggled Squiggle.

'Now see what you've done,' moaned Splodge. 'You've spoiled our jumping. If you're going to be silly, Squiggle, then please don't jump at all.'

Squiggle felt upset. 'I don't like bouncy castles anyway,' she murmured.

Then she went off for a walk on her own.

When we upset someone by being mean, God is upset, too.

What's inside a bouncy castle that makes it so bouncy?

Pens Prayer

Dear Lord, You are always loving and never mean. Thank You. Amen.

Day 23 God Has Feelings, Too

'You do yourself a favour when you are kind.'
(Proverbs 11 v 17)

'I can't see her anywhere,' said Philippa. 'We must all go and look for her.'

'But Rowena and I are having fun bouncing on the bouncy castle,' complained Splodge. 'We don't want to get off now.'

'*I* don't mind,' said Rowena kindly. 'I think it's more important to find Squiggle. I know you didn't mean to, Splodge, but you have been leaving her out a bit today. It'll cheer her up when she knows you've been looking for her.'

When we show someone we care about them, we show God that we care about Him, too.

Why do you think Splodge has been leaving Squiggle out?

Pens Prayer

Loving God, when I know someone is sad, please show me what I can do to help. Amen.

Day 24 God Has Feelings, Too

'... forgive anything you may have against anyone, so that your Father in heaven will forgive ... you ...' (Mark 11 v 25)

Sorry Splodge

Now it was Splodge's turn to be upset.

'Poor Squiggle,' she sobbed. 'I've been so mean. I was just really excited that Rowena was coming to the fair with us. What happens if I NEVER SEE SQUIGGLE AGAIN?'

'Of course, you'll see Squiggle again!' smiled Gloria.

'And when you *do* see her,' added Charlotte, 'you can tell her you're sorry.'

'There she is *now*!' squealed Rowena.

Splodge ran to Squiggle and gave her a big hug. 'I'm so sorry, Squiggle!' she cried. 'I didn't mean to be unkind.'

'That's all right,' smiled Squiggle. 'Thanks for coming to find me.'

When we make up with each other after a quarrel, we make up with God, too.

If you ever have a quarrel with someone, who can you ask to help you sort it out?

Pens Prayer

Dear God, if I quarrel with anyone, please help me to be quick to make friends again. Amen.

Day 25

'When the Son of Man comes as King ... he will sit on his royal throne ...' (Matthew 25 v 31)

When Jesus comes back

'One day,' Jesus told His special friends, 'everyone in the world will see Me again. I will come back as King of the whole earth and I'll sit on My royal throne. People from every country will stand in front of Me.'

Then Jesus said, 'I will put everyone into two groups. I'll ask one group to stand on My right-hand side. I'll ask the other group to stand on My left-hand side.'

No one knows when, but one day Jesus will come back to earth.

Pens Prayer

Thank You, Lord Jesus, that one day I will see You face to face! Amen.

The Good Life

Making God happy

Day 26

'Come and possess the kingdom which has been prepared for you ...' (Matthew 25 v 34)

The Special Place

Jesus' friends listened carefully to everything He said to them. Jesus was their Teacher.

He helped them to understand how much God loved them.

He explained to them how they could be God's friends.

Jesus said, 'I will speak to the group of people on My right-hand side first. I will say to them, "God loves you and is very pleased with you. He has made a special place for you in His kingdom. Come and live there now."'

God invites His friends who love Him to live with Him forever.

Pens Prayer

Thank You so much, Father God, that there is a special place for me in Your kingdom. Amen.

The Good Life

Making God happy

Day 27

'I was hungry and you fed me, thirsty and you gave me a drink ...' (Matthew 25 v 35)

Kind People

Jesus smiled at His friends.

'When I come to earth again,' He said to them, 'I will have more things to say to the people standing on My right-hand side. I will tell them, "When I was hungry, you gave Me something to eat. When I was thirsty, you gave Me something to drink. When I was a stranger, you welcomed Me into your homes. When I had nothing to wear, you gave Me clothes to put on. When I wasn't well, you looked after Me. When I was in prison, you came to see Me."'

God is pleased when we care for each other.

Pens Prayer

Dear Lord, please help me to be caring towards other people. Amen.

Day 28

'The righteous will then answer him, "When, Lord, did we ever see you hungry and feed you ...?"' (Matthew 25 v 37)

Good and loving things

Jesus carried on teaching His special friends.

'When I've finished speaking to the people on My right,' Jesus said, 'they will reply, "But when did we see that You were hungry and give You something to eat? When did we see You thirsty and give You something to drink? When did we see You a stranger and welcome You? Or not well and look after You? Or in prison and come and see You?"

'Then I will say to them, "Whenever you did good and loving things for other people, you did good and loving things for Me."'

When we show love and kindness to other people, we're showing love and kindness to Jesus, and to our Father God.

Pens Prayer

Thank You, Lord Jesus, for teaching me how to live the way God wants me to. Amen.

The Good Life

Making God happy

Day 29

'Then he will say to those on his left, "... I was hungry but you would not feed me ..."' (Matthew 25 vv 41–42)

Unkind People

Jesus said to His friends, 'When I have finished speaking to the people on My right-hand side, I will talk to the people on My left. I will say to them, "You've made God very unhappy.

"When I was hungry, you wouldn't give Me food. When I was thirsty, you wouldn't give Me a drink. When I was a stranger, you wouldn't welcome Me into your homes. When I had nothing to wear, you wouldn't give Me any clothes. When I wasn't well, you wouldn't take care of Me. When I was in prison, you wouldn't visit Me."'

In the Bible, God commands us to love each other.

Pens Prayer

Loving Lord, I'm sorry for days when I feel grumpy and I'm unkind. Amen.

The Good Life
Making God happy
Day 30

'... whenever you refused to help one of these least important ones, you refused to help me.' (Matthew 25 v 45)

The wrong way

Jesus' friends saw that He looked sad.

'When I've finished speaking to the people on My left,' Jesus said, 'they will reply, "But when wouldn't we give You food or something to drink? When wouldn't we welcome You, or look after You, or visit You?"

'Then I will say to them, "Whenever you wouldn't help other people, you wouldn't help Me. That makes God very sad."'

God's way is the perfect way to live our lives.

Pens Prayer

Here I am, Father God. Please show me how I can be kind and helpful every day. Amen.

Pens for special times.

An exciting short story plus 5 days of Bible-reading notes

by Alexa Tewkesbury

32-page full colour booklets, 148x148mm and as animated downloads

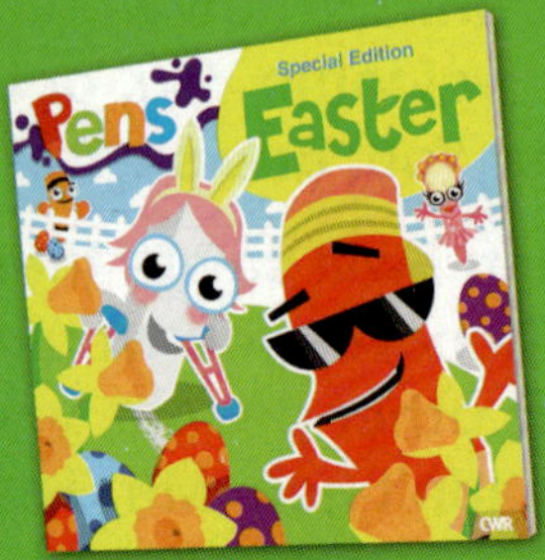

Easter

Help young children understand the true meaning of Easter.

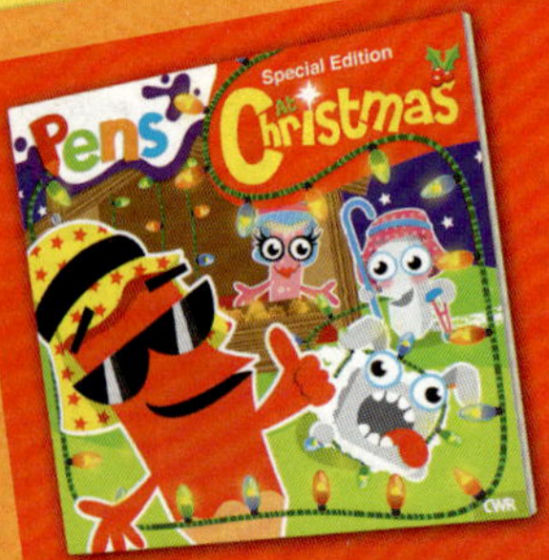

Christmas

The *Pens* characters tell the Christmas story to make Jesus' birth real and memorable for young children.

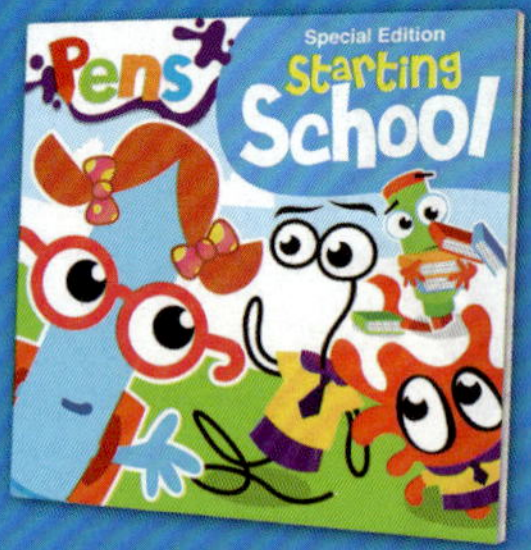

Starting School

Help children start school confidently, knowing that God goes there with them.

Available online, or from Christian bookshops.

For current prices or for animated downloads visit **www.cwr.org.uk/store**